CONTENTS

Some words are shown in bold, **like this**. You can find out what they mean by looking in the glossary.

TAKING TO THE AIR

On 1 September 1939, the German army invaded Poland. World War II had begun. The skies from Europe to the Pacific became filled with warplanes, and fighter pilots fought high-speed duels.

Britain, France, Australia, Canada, and other nations joined the war against Germany in 1939, and against Italy in 1940. And when Japanese planes bombed the US naval base at Pearl Harbor in Hawaii on 7 December 1941, the United States was brought into the war.

Fighter pilots at war

World War II lasted six years, until 1945. It was fought across Europe, North Africa, and Asia – on land, at sea, and in the air. In this global war, aircraft were powerful weapons. Nations had begun preparing for war in the 1930s and in Germany, the **Nazi** leader Adolf Hitler had secretly built a strong air force, the Luftwaffe. By 1939, some pilots already had battle experience. German pilots had fought in the Spanish Civil War (1936–1939), and Japanese pilots had seen combat in China. Some pilots who had flown in World War I (1914–1918), such as Germany's air chief Hermann Goering, believed air power would win the new war.

▲ Until the late 1930s, most fighter planes were biplanes like this US Curtiss P-6 Hawk. Its top speed was about 319 km/h (198 mph), and its pilot fired two machine guns.

4

1935	1935	March 1936
The Luftwaffe is formed in Nazi Germany. Young pilots train secretly at glider clubs.	First test flights of the British Hurricane and German Bf 109 fighters. Both are monoplanes, and faster than the biplanes already in use.	First test flight of the Spitfire, a fighter designed by R. J. Mitchell for Britain's Royal Air Force.

▲ In 1937, new Messerschmitt Bf 109 fighters were flown in Spain by German pilots of the Condor Legion. Nazi Germany helped the anti-government side in the Spanish Civil War.

The age of the fighter

Air-war experts thought **bombers** would destroy armies, navies, and cities, unless fighter planes could intercept the bombers and drive them from the skies. For defence against bombers, air forces hurriedly ordered more fighter planes. In World War II, fighter pilots were destined to play a key role. As war approached and nations built up their air forces, young pilots were trained and factories speeded up production of fighter planes ready for the battles ahead.

New fighters

- In the 1930s, fighter planes were also known as pursuit planes.

- Most fighters had one pilot, though some had an extra crewman to fire guns.

- They had piston engines that turned propellers.

- Biplane (two-wing) fighters had top speeds around 400 km/h (250 mph).

- By 1935 new monoplane (single-wing) fighters could fly at over 480 km/h (300 mph).

5

1937

German pilots fly Bf 109 fighters in Spain. Ace pilot Werner Molders works out new air combat tactics, with pilots using radio for instant communication.

April 1937

German planes bomb the town of Guernica, in Spain. The world is shocked by the destruction.

1 September 1939

Germany invades Poland, starting World War II. The German air force uses over 1,000 planes to attack Poland.

Learning to fly

Many fighter pilots began training straight from school or university. Alongside them were older pilots who had flown before the war at weekends with volunteer military units or with flying clubs.

Basic training

Trainee pilots learned the basics in a slow, two-seat training plane, with an instructor sitting behind. Everyone wanted to "fly solo" (fly alone). Most pilots flew solo after 10 or 12 hours with an instructor. Training included "blind" flying at night – relying on the plane's instruments to work out what was happening! After 16 to 20 more weeks practice, the best pilots were ready to fly a fast fighter.

First flight in a fighter

Nervously, the young pilot would squeeze into the single-seat **cockpit**. He would take hold of the **control column** to prepare for take-off. Once all the pre-flight checks had been made, he would be ready to go. With engine roaring and propeller whirling, the plane would bump across the airfield, to face into the wind. When the pilot opened the throttle, the fighter would accelerate, its tail lift, and then it would rise into the sky. Now all the pilot had to do was to start learning how to survive at war!

▶ US Navy pilot David McCampbell in his Hellcat fighter. He joined the Navy in 1934, trained as a fighter pilot, and flew from aircraft carriers. He did not fly in combat until 1943, when he was 33, which was old for a fighter pilot. On 24 October 1944, Commander McCampbell shot down nine Japanese aircraft in one day – a record by a US pilot. He ended the war with 34 victories.

◄ Pilots in flying kit. Every flying helmet had a radio and an oxygen mask fitted to it. Many people thought fighter pilots were glamorous heroes. Other pilots might laugh at "show-off fighter boys", but everyone knew how brave they were.

Eyewitness

Fighter planes were cramped. With the canopy closed, some pilots felt shut in after open-cockpit training planes. Trainee RAF (Royal Air Force) pilot Johnnie Johnson found his Spitfire a tight squeeze. "You'll soon get used to it," said his instructor, "it's surprising how small you can get when a German is on your tail!" Armour plating and toughened glass gave the pilot some protection, but he knew his plane could break up in seconds if hit by gunfire from an enemy plane.

Vital fighter tasks

- Pursuing and shooting down enemy fighters
- Defending cities from enemy bombers
- Escorting friendly bombers to their targets
- Reconnaissance – taking photos of the enemy
- Sometimes, attacking targets on the ground.

▶ In 1939, the sturdy Hurricane was the RAF's most common fighter. A new pilot had to learn fast. He needed to watch the sky for enemy aircraft, and keep his eye on his instruments – altimeter (height), airspeed indicator (speed) and fuel gauge. And he had to fire his guns at a target whizzing past at great speed.

7

SQUADRON LIFE

New pilots joined a fighter squadron. Each squadron was like a team, and its pilots felt proud to belong to it.

All the nations at war had air forces. Britain's Royal Air Force, like Australia's, was separate from the Navy and Army. The Royal Navy had its own fliers, in the Fleet Air Arm. American fighter pilots flew with the United States Army Air Force or with the US Navy and Marine Corps.

Organization

Air forces were made up of squadrons or groups of aircraft. Each squadron had its own name, number, and badge. A fighter squadron had between eight and twelve fighters. On the airfield, pilots and ground crew lived in huts or tents, receiving their orders from the squadron's commanding officer.

▲ A fighter pilot relied on his ground crew to prepare his plane. Often this meant the mechanics worked all night, making repairs by torchlight. Many pilots took great care of their planes. They would have the guns set to fire at a certain angle to give them the best chance of hitting an enemy.

A team effort

Behind every pilot was a vital support team on the ground. Mechanics serviced the planes between every "op" (operation, or mission). They patched up holes in the **fuselage** or tail, checked the engines, filled fuel tanks, and reloaded guns.

Radar operators on the ground kept lookout for enemy planes. At fighter headquarters, senior officers studied large maps, on which enemy and friendly planes were shown by markers. They ordered fighters into battle, by radio or telephone. Seven of every ten air force personnel worked in ground jobs, and many ground crew were women.

1939	16 October 1939	April 1940
New planes need testing. In April 1939, the new Japanese Zero fighter flies for the first time.	A Spitfire fighter shoots down a German Junkers 88 over Scotland – the first German plane shot down over Britain in World War II.	Germany invades Denmark and Norway. The German fighters are too good for the British warplanes sent to help the Norwegians.

▶ This is a US Air Force recruitment poster from 1940. Other posters featured air force pilots. One such pilot was Peter Parrott, age 20, from the RAF. After just four weeks flying a Hurricane, on 10 May 1940 he shot down his first German bomber, over France. His poster was meant to boost morale, but when Peter saw it he just felt embarrassed!

WINGS OVER AMERICA

AIR CORPS U.S. ARMY

Eyewitness

In 1940, before the United States was in the war, US pilot James Goodson was one of many Americans who volunteered to fight the Nazis. The British recruiting sergeant told him "it will be 21 shillings [£1.05, then 5 US dollars] a week" (meaning the wages). James said he didn't think he could afford to pay that much – which made everyone laugh. American pilots flew fighters in three RAF "Eagle" squadrons during the early part of the war.

◀ These RAF pilots are posing next to their squadron badge. Pilots were posted, or moved, from one squadron to another, sometimes overseas. New pilots joined a squadron to replace men who had left – or who had been killed, wounded, or reported "missing in action".

May–June 1940

The German air force plays a key part in the Nazi conquest of Belgium, the Netherlands, and France.

July–Sept 1940

The Battle of Britain is fought over southern England between RAF fighters and Luftwaffe bombers and fighters.

26 October 1940

First test flight of the NA-73, which becomes the P-51 Mustang, one of the best US fighters of the war.

Off duty

Air combat was exhausting. After each safe landing, pilots reported any enemy aircraft destroyed or damaged. Then they tried to relax.

Many Allied pilots were overseas. For them, "home" was a desert airstrip in Africa or a patch of cleared jungle on a Pacific island. For Navy and Marine pilots, "home" was an aircraft carrier, in the middle of the ocean.

Passing the time

Most of the time, pilots just waited for the next **dogfight**. They spent their off-duty hours eating, sleeping, chatting, playing games, listening to records or to the radio. Someone might find a ball for a game of football or baseball. Pilots read books and magazines, studied, or wrote letters home. Some walked their dogs (dogs were favourite squadron mascots) or played cards, dominoes, or darts. In the evening, pilots stationed in Britain might stroll to the nearest public house or race off in cars or motorbikes to the nearest town to the local cinema or dance. Pilots on leave (with two or more days off) might visit their families.

► A good meal was often hard to find in wartime Britain, because many foods such as meat, sugar, and eggs were rationed. People had ration books, like this, containing coupons to hand over in food shops. Restaurants often had little on the menu to tempt aircrew off duty.

◀ Pilots wore uniform even when off duty: air force blue or, for USAAF crew, pale brown. Fighter pilots were known for their casual dress – RAF pilots left their top jacket button undone. Many wore silk scarves. The scarf stopped the pilot's neck becoming sore as he twisted his head while flying. A leather flying jacket and leather boots with wool linings helped keep the pilot warm.

Eyewitness

RAF pilot Hugh Dundas, fighting in the Battle of Britain, wrote letters to his parents and to his brother John, also a fighter pilot. "I will be on forty-eight hours leave from 30 September to 2 October so if you will let me know where you will be ... I will try to organize myself to be there too." He added that after a day spent flying fighter patrols, "you don't feel like doing more than drinking a spot of dinner and going to bed".

From a letter from Hugh Dundas to his brother John, 25 September 1940. In November, John Dundas was killed in action.

▼ Every pilots' hut had a gramophone (record-player), often a wind-up kind that played one record at a time. Popular music included songs (sentimental and cheery) and dance music played by bands such as the US Army Air Force band led by Glenn Miller.

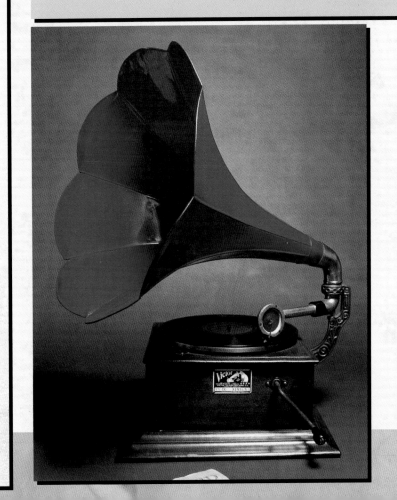

SCRAMBLE!

SCRAMBLE!

The signal for pilots to "scramble" (dash for their planes) came almost every day during the summer of 1940, during the Battle of Britain. This was one of the first major air battles of World War II.

Air battles over Britain

Britain's top-secret radar stations gave 20 minutes' warning of enemy aircraft approaching. When they were detected, it was time to scramble! Pilots dashed to their planes, took off, and climbed high and fast. When they spotted a formation of enemy aircraft, the fight began, with dozens of planes twisting and turning, chasing, and being chased.

Novices and aces in combat

As pilots were lost, young replacements joined squadrons. An inexperienced pilot tried to stay close to his comrades. On his own, he might become an easy "kill" for a German fighter ace (top pilot). Novice pilots had a 50 per cent chance of being killed in their first five combat missions.

Eyewitness

"The losses of aircraft could be made up, but the experienced men ... could not be replaced."

Ulrich Steinhilper, Luftwaffe pilot.

▲ Pilots scramble to their Hurricanes. The Hurricane's Rolls Royce Merlin engine burned petroleum-based fuel, like a car engine. Battle of Britain Spitfires and Hurricanes had eight Browning machine guns fitted in the wings.

June 1940	10 July 1940	15 August 1940
Prime Minister Winston Churchill speaks of the "Battle of Britain" about to begin.	Luftwaffe planes attack ships in the English Channel. RAF fighters battle against German Bf 109 and Bf 110 fighters sent to lure them into combat.	Over 1,800 Luftwaffe planes attack Britain in waves. The Germans lose 76 planes: the British claim to have shot down at least 161.

▶ Ground controllers plotted, or marked, the position of RAF fighters and enemy aircraft on large maps. They passed instructions to the pilots by radio.

The battle won

Some planes flew back to base riddled with bullet holes. Others exploded in mid air, or caught fire, spiralling down to crash into fields or in the sea. Lucky pilots baled out and drifted to earth on parachutes. Back at base, returning pilots counted victories – and the losses – while their planes were hurriedly patched up. The air battles over the airfields of southern England went on into September 1940, when the German air force changed tactics and began bombing London and other cities. This was the start of the **Blitz**. The Battle of Britain had been won by "the few", the RAF's gallant fighter pilots.

Pilots' battle

- The RAF had just over 1,300 fighter pilots when the Battle of Britain began on 10 July 1940.

- They included Britons, Americans, New Zealanders, Canadians, South Africans, Poles, and Czechs.

- During August 1940, over 500 RAF pilots were killed or wounded. Only 260 new pilots finished training.

- During July–October 1940, the Luftwaffe lost 1,733 aircraft. In the same period, over 900 RAF fighters were shot down or damaged.

13

7 September 1940

After Britain bombs Berlin, German bombers switch their attacks from RAF airfields to London.

15 September 1940

Almost 300 RAF fighters assemble for battle over Kent and London. Around 55 German planes are shot down. The RAF loses about 28.

October 1940

Hitler abandons his plan to invade Britain. Over 1,500 German planes have been shot down in the Battle of Britain.

SCRAMBLE!

In combat

An American pilot described a fighter battle as "like kids running round the block to get away from bullies, always looking behind". Most pilots lived one day at a time.

Advice for the young

Experienced pilots knew that if you flew in a straight line for too long (more than 30 seconds), you made a good target. Confused, frightened, or dazzled by the sun, many newcomers were shot down by enemies they never saw. New pilots were warned not to be "'trigger-happy" and shoot at friends – it was hard to tell one plane from another in high-speed air fighting.

Major George E. Preddy Jr., ace pilot of P-47s and P-51s with the US 8th Air Force in Europe, told new pilots to keep looking around though "it is impossible to see everything …" After 28 victories, he was killed in combat on Christmas Day 1944.

South African A. G. "Sailor" Malan was by 1940 an RAF fighter ace at the age of 30. His ten rules for air fighting included: try to get higher than the enemy, always turn your aircraft to face an attack, always act quickly, and lastly "Go in quickly – punch hard – get out!"

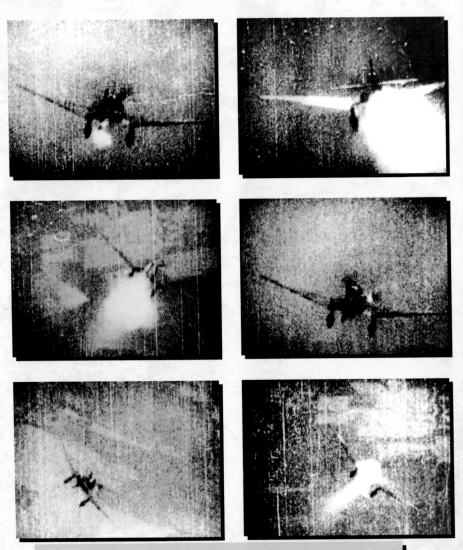

▲ Fighters carried camera guns to film attacks on enemy planes. Here a British pilot destroys a German Ju 87 Stuka dive-bomber. Pilots usually opened fire at a **range** of 150 to 250 metres, but sometimes as close as 50 metres.

14

Fooled you...

To escape pursuing fighters, German fighter ace Adolf Galland would fire his guns at nothing. Smoke and used cartridges would blow back from his plane, fooling the chasing pilot into thinking the German fighter had a backward-firing gun! He would break off the pursuit, giving Galland time to escape.

Pilot-speak

Pilots had their own jargon, often humorous.

- Enemy planes were "bandits"; an unknown radar blip was an "angel".

- A "bogey" might be friend or foe.

- If a pilot "ditched", he'd crashed into the sea.

- If a pilot "bought it", he was dead.

- An enemy plane shot down was "destroyed" or a "kill"; one damaged was a "possible" or "probable".

▲ Billy Fiske, the first American pilot to die in combat in World War II. He joined the RAF in 1939 and died in August 1940 after his Hurricane crashed in Sussex. A plaque in St Paul's Cathedral, London remembers him as "An American citizen who died that England might live". Nine US pilots fought in the Battle of Britain in 1940.

▲ US P-38 Lightning fighter planes patrol the skies in 1942. One pilot wrote of "crossing white trails in the blue sky ..." [the vapour trails from aircraft engines], and enemy planes appearing as "a string of tiny silhouettes against a distant cloud".

FIGHTERS ON ALL FRONTS

By 1941, pilots were fighting in the Mediterranean and in the Soviet Union. Then, after the attack on Pearl Harbor in December 1941, US pilots had to pit their courage and skill against Japanese fighters.

Naval fighters

In the Pacific war, the **Allies** and the Japanese used aircraft carriers as mobile airfields at sea. US Navy pilots flew many miles across the oceans to attack enemy ships and planes. In air battles against Japanese pilots, the Americans used the greater speed of their fighters, such as the USAAF's twin-engined P-38 Lightning (around 627 km/h – 390 mph) and the US Navy's F6F Hellcat (612 km/h – 380 mph).

The Japanese A6M Zero fighter was fairly fast (534 km/h – 332 mph) and had a long range, but it did not have steel armour and it caught fire easily. The Ki-61 Hien was better, because it had armour and fuel tanks that sealed themselves if hit. Unlike the Americans, Japanese pilots did not have radios. Instead, they signalled to one another by hand waves or by waggling the plane's wings. Few Japanese pilots carried a parachute either: they thought it a disgrace to be taken prisoner.

Escorting bombers

Fighters were also used to escort bombers. In Europe, the Allies launched massive air raids on Germany, the RAF bombing by night and the USAAF by day. Darkness hid the bombers, though German night-fighter pilots used radar to track them. By day, German fighters shot down many US bombers, which at first flew over Germany without fighter escorts. By 1944, the Americans had a fighter that could fly from Britain to Germany and back – the P-51D version of the Mustang.

▼ This German Bf 110 night-fighter was fitted with radar to guide its pilot to a target in the darkness.

June 1941	7 December 1941	1942
German armies invade the Soviet Union. Soviet pilots include women – the only women pilots in combat in WW II.	Japanese planes flying from aircraft carriers attack US Navy ships at Pearl Harbor, Hawaii. The United States then enters the war.	Fighter planes are in action over the deserts of North Africa and in the Mediterranean, especially around the island of Malta.

▲ The P-51D Mustang was very fast, could climb to 12,500 m (40,000 ft) and fly for over 2,400 km (1,500 miles). "When I saw Mustangs over Berlin, I knew the war was lost," said Hermann Goering, head of the Luftwaffe.

Eyewitness

"If you are jumped [attacked] from above, dive to pick up a speed of at least 350 mph [563 km/h], then level out and start a shallow climb at high airspeed. Generally speaking, a Japanese fighter will not follow you in a high-speed dive ..."

Advice from Major Richard Bong, the leading US ace in the Pacific with 40 victories. He saw action from November 1942 to December 1944 but was killed in August 1945 test-flying a P-80 jet fighter.

Major air battles	Key Allied fighters	Key Axis* fighters
France 1940	Hurricane	Bf 109
Britain 1940	Hurricane, Spitfire	Bf 109, Bf 110,
China, Philippines 1940–1941	P-39 Airacobra, P-40 Tomahawk	Zero
North Africa 1941–1942	P-40 Tomahawk, Hurricane, Spitfire	Bf 109, CR42
Russia 1941–1943	I-16, La-3, MiG-3	Bf 109, Fw 190
Malta 1942	Gladiator, Hurricane, Spitfire	CR42, Bf 109
Germany 1943–1945	P-51 Mustang, P-47 Thunderbolt	Fw 190, Me 262
Normandy 1944	P-51 Mustang, Spitfire, Typhoon	Bf 109, Fw 190
Pacific 1941–1945	F6F Hellcat, P-38 Lightning, F4U Corsair	Zero, Ki-43, Ki-61, Ki-84

*The Axis was the wartime alliance between Germany, Italy, and Japan

February 1942–November 1943
Australian Spitfire pilots fight off Japanese attacks on Darwin, in northern Australia.

June 1942–February 1943
US naval aircraft play a key role in the Pacific battle of Midway and in air battles over Guadalcanal in the Solomon Islands.

May 1944
Long-range US P-51D Mustangs begin escorting Allied bombers as far as Berlin, capital of Germany.

Fighting far from home

For a pilot on a carrier in the Pacific Ocean or on a tiny airfield in the middle of the jungle, home seemed far away. Thousands of Allied pilots flew overseas. For most, it was their first time in a foreign country. American and Commonwealth pilots based in Britain missed steaks and ice cream, but came to enjoy pubs, games of darts, and being invited to tea with British families.

Roughing it

Pilots wondered which was worse: jungle or desert. Both were too hot. In the jungle, the rainy season soaked everything, planes got stuck in mud, and insects got everywhere. In the desert, sand blew into aircraft and clothes. Sometimes, pilots in faraway places felt forgotten – they often did not get the best aircraft. The P-40 Tomahawk, not good enough for air battles in Europe, was sent to North Africa and China. RAF pilots in the desert liked its big US-style cockpit, but not the smelly smoke blown back in their faces whenever the guns were fired.

Eyewitness

In Burma, one RAF pilot remembered, "it was nasty and inhospitable jungle ... but there were relaxations. There were jeep races – the squadrons turned up in their favourite jeeps and raced them round a course. The betting was usually heavy as there was not too much to spend money on ..."

▶ This leaflet welcomed American servicemen to Britain, explaining the kind of country – and people – they were going to meet.

Welcome!

◀ An F6F Hellcat of the US Navy. Hellcats first saw action in August 1943, flying from the carrier *USS Yorktown*. More than 2,500 Hellcats were built during 1943 alone.

Keeping up spirits

- Wherever they were, pilots looked forward to letters from home. Their own letters were **censored** (the pilots were not allowed to say where they were, or what they were doing).

- The squadrons published their own newspapers, full of complaints, cartoons, and jokes about the enemy.

- Most fliers kept up their spirits with concerts and games of football or baseball.

▼ As the war ebbed and flowed, pilots often had to move quickly from one airstrip to another.

19

SHOT DOWN

In combat, a fighter could be shot at by enemy planes or by anti-aircraft guns on the ground. Some pilots were shot down by their own side. Lucky pilots escaped by crash-landing damaged planes or jumping out, using a parachute.

Missing in action

Some planes just disappeared, their pilots reported "missing in action". Getting lost, running out of fuel, and engine failure could all cause a crash. Some crashes were caused by pilot "blackouts". In high-speed twists and dives, a fighter pilot's body was stressed by g-forces (increased gravity). He might first "grey out" (feel ill) and then "black out" (become unconscious). If he did not wake up in time, his plane hit the ground or the sea.

Taken prisoner

A crashed pilot hoped to be rescued by his own side. US Marine Corps pilot Gregory "Pappy" Boyington was shot down in his F4U Corsair fighter over New Guinea in January 1944. He parachuted into the ocean. He drifted for some time in his small life raft before eventually being picked up by a Japanese submarine. He became one of many **prisoners of war**.

▶ This German Bf 109 plane was shot down by British fighters over England in 1940 during the Battle of Britain.

April 1941	September 1942	16 August 1943
Flight Lieutenant "Pat" Pattle is killed in Greece, after scoring at least 41 victories – the most by any RAF pilot.	Hans Joachim Marseille, the top German ace in North Africa with 158 victories, is killed aged 21. He bales out of his Bf 109 but his parachute does not open.	Mike Cooper, an RAF Spitfire pilot, is shot down (for the third time), and parachutes into France. He escapes to Britain.

Tales of courage

Some pilots suffered terrible injuries, when fighter planes caught fire. Crashes stopped many pilots flying again, but not all. Famous British pilot Douglas Bader wore artificial legs after a flying accident in 1931. By 1939 he was back in the RAF and leading fighters into battle. His plane crashed in France in 1941 and he was taken prisoner.

Eyewitness

Desmond Sheen, an Australian fighter pilot with the RAF, was shot down during the Battle of Britain. "I released my safety straps, turned the Spitfire on its back ... and went out as clean as a whistle. My parachute opened at 10,000 ft [3,000m] ... and I had a grandstand view of the battle." Four days later in 1940, Sheen was shot down again. He parachuted into a wood, seconds before his plane crashed.

▲ A pilot shot down into the sea floated in his lifejacket or in a small inflatable rubber raft. Many pilots ended up in this situation. Rescue teams in planes or boats tried to find them – pilots were too valuable to lose.

May 8 1944

Robert Johnson completes his 91st combat mission in 11 months with his 28th victory. He returns home as the top American ace in Europe.

November 5 1944

US Navy pilot David McCampbell ends his combat "tour" in the Pacific having destroyed 34 Japanese planes.

7 January 1945

Major Tommy McGuire (USAAF, 38 victories) crashes during an air battle over the Philippines.

Staying alive

Some pilots survived three or more crashes, and most liked to joke about their escapes. Others escaped death, but were scarred for life by injuries.

Escape from fire

Every pilot feared being trapped in a burning plane. In October 1940, George Bennions' RAF Spitfire burst into flames when hit by a German fighter. Blinded in one eye and badly wounded, Bennions fell out and parachuted down into a field. He suffered terrible burns, but his skin was painstakingly repaired by the brilliant and pioneering **plastic surgeon**, Archibald McIndoe, whose medical team treated many fliers.

Survival on your own

In some places, local people risked their lives to help Allied pilots. But the worst places to crash-land were in the desert, jungle, or Pacific Ocean. Desert fliers were told "always fly in the boots you intend to use to walk home", and to walk at night and rest in shade during the day. Pilots carried a note called a "blood chit" written in several languages, asking local people for help.

In the jungle, a crashed pilot might have to survive for weeks. He had a survival kit that included a machete or jungle knife, torch, compass, water-sterilizing tablets, hooks and a line (for catching fish to eat), soap, razor blade, sewing kit, and matches.

▼ This World War II plane crashed into the jungle in Papua New Guinea. Even if the pilot survived the crash, he would still have faced the difficult task of surviving alone in the jungle.

Eyewitness

"All his eight machine guns went into the right wing and I had to shut down the right engine. Nothing else for it but to go down into the sea ..."

Lieutenant Rudolf Behnisch, German pilot of a Heinkel bomber shot down by a Spitfire over northern England, 1940.

▲ Emergency rations included chocolate, cheese, powdered milk, and tablets to purify water for drinking. Pilots did not know how long rescue would take. The rations in this photo were taken from a Japanese fighter plane.

Escape aids

Escape aids given to pilots included:

- a map printed on silk, hidden in clothing

- a compass small enough to be hidden in a button

- flying boots that could be cut down to look like ordinary shoes

- passport-type photos, for use on fake identity papers.

◀ RAF pilots called their lifejacket a "Mae West" (after a famous film star). It was fitted with a whistle, colour dye markers, knife, battery, and lamp.

23

VICTORY ROLL

By 1944, the Allies were winning the fighter war. All air forces had fighters that were much better than those of 1940, but the Allied factories were building them faster.

The invasion of Europe

On D-Day (6 June 1944) the Allies landed in Normandy, France, to begin the liberation of Western Europe. Fighter planes protected the soldiers and ships, escorted the bombers, and attacked German defences. Low-flying fighters, like the British Typhoon, shot up enemy trucks and trains carrying war supplies, such as fuel. German fighters were out-numbered.

Fighters rule the skies

The Allies sent up to 1,000 bombers at a time to bomb Germany, escorted by as many as 800 fighters. Swarms of fighters supported the Soviet armies attacking Germany from the east. The German air force needed 160,000 tonnes of fuel oil a month. By September 1944, it was getting fewer than 20,000 tonnes and many German fighters were kept on the ground with empty fuel tanks.

In the Pacific, the Japanese air force was also running out of fuel and pilots. Bombers destroyed Japanese air bases. As Allied forces drew closer to Japan, Japanese *kamikaze* pilots flew suicide missions, crashing their planes deliberately into US and British ships.

▲ A *kamikaze* attack on a US warship. This Japanese plane is about to crash into the USS *Missouri* battleship.

6 June 1944	1944	June 1944
D-Day, the Allies land in Normandy to begin the liberation of Western Europe.	German Me 262 **jets** go into action. Hitler orders many to be used as fighter-bombers, which slows them down.	German V-1 flying bombs are launched at Britain. Fighters shoot down many of the pilotless "doodlebugs" over the English Channel.

Oil supplies in 1944

- Germany 9.5 million tonnes
- Japan 1 million tonnes
- USA 222 million tonnes

Aircraft production (all types) in 1944

- Germany 40,000
- Japan 29,000
- United States 96,000
- UK 26,000
- USSR 40,000

▲ German and Japanese aircraft factories went on working, despite the Allied bombing. But Allied factories made more fighters faster. And the Allies were not losing as many pilots. By 1945 most of the best German and Japanese pilots were dead.

Eyewitness

Toshiro Ohmura started flying training in Japan in 1942 and became an operational pilot in July 1944. In a last letter to his father in July 1945 he wrote, "I believe it is a great honour for me, aged 18, to die as a suicide attack pilot ... I shall die smiling." He was killed when his plane crashed into the sea close to the aircraft carrier he was attacking. A week later the war was over.

4 August 1944
An RAF Meteor jet fighter destroys a V-1 by tipping it over with its wingtip – the first success for Britain's new jet.

October 1944
Battle of Leyte Gulf in the Pacific, fought mainly between US and Japanese carrier-launched planes. The US Navy wins a crucial victory.

25 October 1944
The first Japanese suicide attack: 24 volunteer *kamikaze* pilots fly Zero fighters to hit US warships.

Technology advancing

In 1944 the German and Japanese air forces were short of planes, fuel, and pilots. But Germany had some new secret weapons, including the V-1 flying bomb, and the world's first combat jet fighter, the Me 262.

Jet fighters roar into battle

With a speed of over 850 km/h (528 mph), the twin-jet Me 262 was 150 km/h (93 mph) faster than a P-51 Mustang. The only way Allied pilots could hit it was to swoop from above at maximum speed, and shoot before the German plane sped away.

In 1944 Britain's new jet fighter, the Meteor, was hurried into action to attack V-1 flying bombs. Ten thousand V-1s were launched from German bases in France. Luckily, only about 3,500 hit targets in England. People called them "buzz bombs" or "doodlebugs", from the droning sound of their engines – which cut out when the bombs had reached the target zone.

▲ The V-1 was a pilotless plane, with a jet engine and a nose packed with explosives. It flew as fast as the fastest propeller-fighter. Allied fighter pilots shot down V-1s or tipped them over, so the flying bombs crashed harmlessly.

The end of the war

Despite its new hi-tech weapons, by May 1945 Germany was defeated. The war in Europe was over. Japan continued to resist, still sending suicide pilots to their deaths, until August 1945, when the Allies dropped **atomic bombs** that destroyed the cities of Hiroshima and Nagasaki. Japan surrendered and the Pacific war ended.

▶ US soldiers with a captured Me 262 jet fighter. German pilot Heinz Bar had 16 victories in a Me 262, out of his wartime total of 220.

◄ By August 1945, the war was over. Thousands of fighter planes stood silent on airfields all over the world. These airmen were on parade at Castle Camps airfield in Cambridgeshire, England, to mark the Allied victory. As fighter pilots joined in the victory parties, they remembered those who had died. Many also started thinking about a job in peacetime.

Some famous fighters of the war

	Top speed	Weapons
Hawker Hurricane I (1940, UK)	499 km/h (310 mph)	8 machine guns
Mitsubishi A6M2 Zero (1940, Japan)	534 km/h (332 mph)	3 machine guns, 2 cannon
Messerschmitt Bf 110C (1940, Germany)	561 km/h (349 mph)	4 machine guns, 2 cannon
Supermarine Spitfire V (1941, UK)	594 km/h (369 mph)	8 machine guns or 4 cannon
Messerschmitt Bf 109F (1941, Germany)	600 km/h (373 mph)	2 machine guns, 2 cannon
Grumman Hellcat (1943, United States)	612 km/h (380 mph)	6 machine guns
Focke Wulf Fw190A-3 (1941, Germany)	673 km/h (418 mph)	2 machine guns, 2 cannon
Republic P-47B Thunderbolt (1942, United States)	697 km/h (433 mph)	8 machine guns
North American P-51D Mustang (1943, United States)	703 km/h (437 mph)	6 machine guns
Messerschmitt Me 262 (1944, Germany)	869 km/h (540 mph)	4 cannon

Note: fighters were also adapted to carry rockets and bombs, for attacking ground targets.

FRIENDS AFTER FIGHTING

Fighter pilots earned a place of honour among the heroes of World War II. In peacetime, former enemies became friends and talked over their experiences. Some still meet today.

After 1945, air force pilots switched from propellers to jets. US ace Francis "Gabby" Gabreski, with 31 wartime victories, added 6 more flying jet fighters in the Korean War (1950–1953). Many pilots took jobs flying airliners or cargo planes.

Mutual respect

Pilots from both sides met to swap memories. There was mutual respect. "I shot at aircraft, I didn't shoot at people," said one RAF pilot. The aircraft they flew can be seen in museums, and a few World War II fighters still fly, preserved as tributes to the brave men who fought in them.

Fighter aces of World War II

An ace was a pilot who had destroyed five or more enemy aircraft.

Erich Hartmann (Germany)	352
Hiroyoshi Nishizawa (Japan)	85+
Ivan Kozhedub (USSR)	62
Richard Bong (United States)	41
M. T. St.J. Pattle (S Africa)	40
J. E. Johnson (UK)	38
G. F. Beurling (Canada)	31
C. R. Caldwell (Australia)	28½
C. F. Gray (New Zealand)	27½
Adriano Visconti (Italy)	26

After the war

- Johannes Steinhof, a Me 262 ace, later flew with the post-war West German air force.

- Neville Duke, with 28 wartime victories in the RAF, set a world air speed record of 1,170 km/h (727 mph), in a Hunter jet in 1953.

- Robin Olds flew P-38s and P-51s with the US 8th Air Force. In 1967, at the age of 45, he piloted a supersonic F-4 Phantom jet during the Vietnam War.

▶ Stan Josefiak was a Polish pilot who flew for the RAF during the Battle of Britain in 1940. He is pictured here wearing his medals at a memorial service for Polish airmen in 2000, 55 years after the end of the war.

FRIENDS AFTER FIGHTING

TIMELINE

1939

1 September Germany invades Poland. World War II begins.

3 September Britain and France declare war on Germany. British aircraft production leaps from 2,153 in 1937 to 7,940 in 1939. British fighter pilots move to France, ready for combat.

October An RAF Spitfire shoots down the first German bomber destroyed over Britain.

1940

April Germany invades Denmark and Norway.

May Germans invade Belgium, the Netherlands and France, with fighters supporting ground troops in "*Blitzkrieg*" (lightning war) attacks.

May The British army is evacuated from Dunkirk, France.

June Italy joins Germany in the Axis alliance. On June 17, France stops fighting.

July The Japanese Navy starts flying its new Zero fighters.

July The German air force (Luftwaffe) sets out to destroy Britain's Royal Air Force.

August The Battle of Britain is at its height.

September Big German air raids on London. The Luftwaffe gives up its attempt to defeat the RAF.

1941

April Germany invades Greece and Yugoslavia.

June Germany invades the Soviet Union. Many German pilots eventually score 150 or more victories against the slower Russian planes.

7 December The Japanese attack on Pearl Harbor, Hawaii brings the United States into the war. Soon after, Britain, Canada, and Australia declare war on Japan, and Germany declares war on the United States.

1942

February Singapore and Malaya fall to Japan. Japanese planes sink two Royal Navy warships, which have no air cover.

19 February Japanese planes raid northern Australia.

May Battle of the Coral Sea between US and Japanese carrier-launched aircraft. There is no clear winner.

June Battle of Midway in the Pacific. Japan loses four aircraft carriers and many pilots to US Navy planes.

August–February German and Russian armies fight for Stalingrad in the Soviet Union.

November Helped by growing air power, the Allies defeat Axis forces at El Alamein in North Africa.

November More Allied armies land in North Africa.

1943

January The Allies begin bombing Germany night and day, with fighters escorting bombers on daylight raids. German night fighters shoot down many RAF bombers.

April Alerted by code-breakers, US P-38 fighters shoot down a plane carrying Japanese Admiral Yamamoto, mastermind of the Pearl Harbor raid in 1941.

July The Allies land in Sicily, and invade mainland Italy in September. The Pacific War also turns in favour of the Allies.

1944

March US bombers raid Berlin by day. P-51 Mustangs escort the bombers and hunt German fighters.

6 June D-Day; Allied armies invade Normandy in France to begin the liberation of Western Europe. Allied planes control the skies over the battle zone.

June The Germans fire the first V-1 flying bombs against Britain. Tempests and Meteor jets are the only RAF fighters fast enough to shoot them down.

September V-2 attacks begin on London. Fighters are no defence against these faster-than-sound rockets.

October A B-17 bomber is shot down by a German jet fighter – the first loss to a Me 262. Germany uses rockets for air-to-air attacks on bombers.

October American ships and pilots in the Pacific win the Battle of Leyte Gulf, the biggest naval-air battle of the war.

25 October The first *kamikaze* attacks are launched by Japan, which sacrifices thousands of planes and pilots in suicide missions up to August 1945.

1945

February US forces land on Iwo Jima island, closing in on Japan.

30 April Adolf Hitler kills himself as Soviet armies destroy Berlin. The Luftwaffe has very few planes or pilots left, and little fuel.

April American forces land on Okinawa, close to the main Japanese islands.

7 May Germany surrenders.

8 May People celebrate VE (Victory in Europe) Day.

6 August The Allies drop an atomic bomb on Hiroshima and another on Nagasaki three days later.

14 August V-J (Victory over Japan) Day ends the war, though the official Japanese surrender is not until 2 September.

GLOSSARY

Allies nations joining forces to fight an enemy. In WWII the Allies were the United States, France, the Soviet Union (or USSR), and Britain and its Commonwealth partners, such as Canada, Australia, India, and New Zealand.

atomic bomb weapon using nuclear fission to create an explosion of energy more destructive than any bomb used before the 1940s

Blitz the German bombing attack on London and other British cities, beginning in 1940

Blitzkrieg German for "lightning war", fast attacks made by tanks and ground soldiers, supported by aircraft with guns and bombs

bomber plane designed to fly over a target and drop explosive and incendiary (fire-starting) bombs

censored controlled information; letters from military personnel were checked to make sure they contained no information helpful to the enemy

cockpit seating section of a fighter plane. Inside, the pilot sits at the controls, usually protected by an armoured glass canopy.

control column a steering control held in both hands. It also contained a firing button for guns.

dogfight airborne combat between fighter planes

fighter fast plane designed to intercept enemy bombers, and shoot them down with guns or rockets

fuselage the main body of a plane, without the wings and tail

jet engine which sucks in air at one end and shoots out hot gases at the other, driving a plane at high speed

kamikaze Japanese for "divine wind", used to describe pilots who flew suicide missions

Nazis members of the National Socialist German Workers' Party, led by Adolf Hitler

plastic surgeon doctor who repairs damaged skin and bones, for example, rebuilding a face damaged by burns

prisoners of war soldiers, sailors, or aircrew captured in wartime

radar use of radio waves to detect distant objects, invented in the 1930s as "radiolocation"

range the distance between a gun and the target. Also, the distance a plane can fly without needing to land and refuel.

FINDING OUT MORE

If you are interested in finding out more about World War II, here are some more books and websites you might find useful.

Further reading

Your local public library's adult section should have plenty of war books, including books about what it was like to be a fighter pilot during the war. Written by people who were actually there, such books will give you an idea of what these brave men thought about the war and their part in it.

Books for younger readers

Britain at War: Air Raids, Martin Parson (Wayland, 1999)

Causes and Consequences of the Second World War, Stewart Ross (Evans, 2003)

Causes of World War II, Paul Dowswell (Heinemann Library, 2002)

Going to War in World War II, Moira Butterfield (Franklin Watts, 2001)

History Through Poetry; World War II, Reg Grant (Hodder Wayland, 2001)

The Day the War was Won, Colin Hymion (Ticktock Media, 2003)

World in Flames: In the Air, Peter Hepplewhite (Macmillan Children's Books, 2001)

World in Flames: On Land, Neil Tonge (Macmillan Children's Books, 2001)

WW2 Stories: War at Home, Anthony Masters (Franklin Watts, 2004)

WW2 Stories: War in the Air, Anthony Masters (Franklin Watts, 2004)

WW2 True Stories, Clive Gifford (Hodder Children's Books, 2002)

Websites

http://www.iwm.org.uk/ – the website of the Imperial War Museum in London.

http://www.wartimememories.co.uk/ – a website containing wartime recollections, including those of fighter pilots in World War II.

http://bbc.co.uk/history/war/wwtwo/ – this website from the BBC has lots of resources about World War II.

INDEX